The Book Of
ILLUSTRATED PROVERBS

To Jim,
The fountain of wisdom
flows through books.
With a flowing pen.
　　　　Best Wishes,
　　　　Rudy Gallo

RUDY GALLO

GOLDEN SEAL PRESS

For Mary

Printed in the
United States of America
First Printing 1996
ISBN 0-9651918-0-X

Library of Congress Catalog Number 96-76195
Copyright 1996 by Rudy Gallo
103 Buena Vista Avenue
Cambridge, Maryland 21613

CONTENTS

INTRODUCTION iv

ANIMALS AND FOWL 2

PLANES, AUTOS, AND OTHER VEHICLES 24

ART, MUSIC AND DANCE 38

WORK AND CHORES 50

CHILDREN AND FAMILIES 66

PEOPLE AND PLACES 78

FOOD AND DRINK 94

HEALTH 106

EDUCATION 116

LAW 130

FORTUNE AND MISFORTUNE 142

SUN AND WATER 162

ENVIRONMENT 176

LOVE AND FRIENDSHIP 190

RELIGION 204

SPORTS AND GAMES .216

HUMAN INTEREST 234

INDEX 250

ABOUT THE AUTHOR 255

INTRODUCTION

The quest for truth is a characteristic common to every civilization. And the test of truth is its timelessness. Indeed, if a stitch in time saves nine today, it probably did the same thing two centuries ago. Through experience and wisdom, listening and watching, winning and losing, these observations have been handed from one generation to the next. It is a sure bet, people 100 years from now will be reading our contributions to this endless collection. That is the first Rule of Truth: it is limitless.

For more than two centuries these single-sentence statements of fact have been called proverbs. Research into their origin suggests in 4 BC king Solomon may have used stories as a way to gain the confidence of dubious Israelites he was trying to lead. These tales were brief and didactic and, if legend holds true, convincing. Solomon was able to begin trade with other countries and history suggests the simple fact he could make clear not just his goal but the reason for even attempting the goal was due in large part to his use of examples and symbolism to drive home a point. And that is the second Rule of Truth: it is always right in front of you.

Mother Goose has the short story, Aesop has the fable, Moses has the Ten Commandments and, although each comes from very different sides of the street, each carries its version of The Way Things Are. Arriving at these varied conclusions isn't easy. In fact, wars may have been fought before a particular notion began to take shape and become the base upon which lives are led today. The greatest challenge then, the most difficult dilemma, the lowest or highest point in the life experience, all of this can be the stuff of which novels or movies are made, but it is also the marrow of a proverb. The complex is framed into being simple. That which overwhelms is all of a sudden smaller. Wounds don't seem so deep. Anger no longer dictates. This is the third Rule of Truth: it is uncomplicated.

Just as a few words can accomplish what pages attempt, so too can a drawing pull us toward an idea. You are holding a few of the observations whose beginnings go back generations. The illustrations by Rudy Gallo make this wonderful collection of proverbs all the more timeless, obvious and pure.

Phrases
and
Expressions

"Acquaint thyself with proverbs, for of them thou shall learn instruction."
Ecclesiasticus 8,8.

ANIMALS AND FOWL

If you sell the cow you sell her milk too.

Go to bed with the lamb and rise with the lark.

Every dog has his day.

*A*s the old cock crows,
the young one learns.

*I*f all fools wore white caps, we should seem a flock of geese.

*A*n ass is but an ass
though laden with gold.

*H*e *that lives with wolves*
will learn to howl.

A mouse must not think to cast a shadow like an elephant.

*E*very bird must hatch
her own egg.

*E*ven the lion must defend
itself against flies.

*A*n ass is beautiful to an
ass and a pig to a pig.

Do not reckon your chickens before they are hatched.

*T*he ladder become
the former.

*B*irds *of a feather*
flock together.

*All are not thieves
that dogs bark at.*

*D*o not foster animals
with hooked claws.

He who chases two hares catches neither.

A pretty pig makes an ugly old sow.

He that would have eggs must bear with cackling.

*D*o not put the saddle
on the wrong horse.

*W*hen the cat is away,
the mice will play.

*E*very bird is known
by its feathers.

What has a dog to do with a bath?

PLANES, AUTOS, AND OTHER VEHICLES

In a long journey weigh straws.

Put your own shoulder to the wheel.

Slow and steady wins the race.

*L*et the past be past.

*D*eliberating is not delaying.

*A*mbition and love are
the wings of great actions.

*N*othing is impossible
to industry.

*A*dvice when most
needed is least heeded.

The horseshoe that clatters wants a nail.

*T*he things are most dear
to us which cost us most.

*H*e goes far that
never turns.

*N*othing *is invented and perfected at the same time.*

*D*elays *are dangerous.*

*K*now your time.

*S*eize what is highest, and you
will possess what is in between.

ART, MUSIC AND DANCE

Hope is grief's best music.

A good drum does not need hard striking.

In a fiddler's house all are dancers.

*E*very land fosters some
kind of art.

*M*usic is the incitement
of love.

*M*usic is the universal speech.

*C*riticism is easy, and
art is difficult.

*A*rt consist in
concealing art.

*E*verything ancient is
to be respected.

*A*rt has an enemy
called ignorance.

*W*ho loves not wine, woman
and song, remains a fool his
whole life long.

*E*ach bird loves to hear
himself sing.

*P*ractice makes
perfect.

WORK AND CHORES

Every day brings its work.

He that does nothing finds helpers.

Employment brings enjoyment.

*E*lbow grease is the
best polish.

*V*ery great in
small matters.

*T*he highest seat will
not hold two.

*A*ny country supports
the skilled workman.

*T*hings united
are helpful.

Injury serves as a lesson.

*G*reatness is nothing
but many small littles.

*N*ot knowledge,
but practice.

*W*ithout sweat and toil
no work is brought to
completion.

*A*fter the fashion
of our ancestors.

*M*an may bear
till his back breaks.

*A workman is known
by his work.*

*B*eneath one's
dignity.

*T*ake things as you
find them.

CHILDREN AND FAMILIES

A child may have too much of his mother's blessing.

Children and drunken folk speak the truth.

Ask the young people; they know everything.

The mind remains unconquered.

*C*hildren are what you
make them.

*F*or that which is sweet
if it be often repeated
is no longer sweet.

*H*unger is the teacher
of many things.

*G*od made us, and we
admire ourselves.

Willing or unwilling.

*W*hat hands have built
hands can pull down.

Victory loves trouble.

*I*t is human to err.

*B*oys are boys, and boys
employ themselves with
boyish matters.

PEOPLE AND PLACES

As alike as two peas.

Far from home is near to harm.

A constant guest is never welcome.

*A*n *Englishman's house*
is his castle.

*We live not as we desire,
but as we can.*

*G*o into the country and hear
what news is in town.

*O*ften a great man comes forth
from a humble cottage.

*W*hat the mind of man
commands to itself it obtains.

*E*ngland is the paradise
of women.

*E*very couple is not a pair.

A pair well matched.

*O*ne often has need of
someone less than oneself.

*L*et it be given to the
most worthy.

*L*et it stand as an example.

*E*very country has its custom.

*E*veryone is wont to praise
him who is no more.

Country is dear, but liberty dearer still.

FOOD AND DRINK

Eat at pleasure,
drink by measure.

A cook is known by his knife.

I know on which side
my bread is buttered.

*H*unger sweetens beans.

He that has teeth has not bread, he that has bread has not teeth.

*A*ll things require skill
but an appetite.

A mad beast must have a sober driver.

All bread is not baked
in one oven.

*T*hose who are thirsty drink
in silence.

*E*at a bit before you drink.

*T*oo *many cooks spoil the broth.*

*H*e deserves not the sweet that
will not taste of the sour.

A common jar often holds generous nectar.

HEALTH

Every man hath his ill day.

Feed a cold and starve a fever.

Health and money go far.

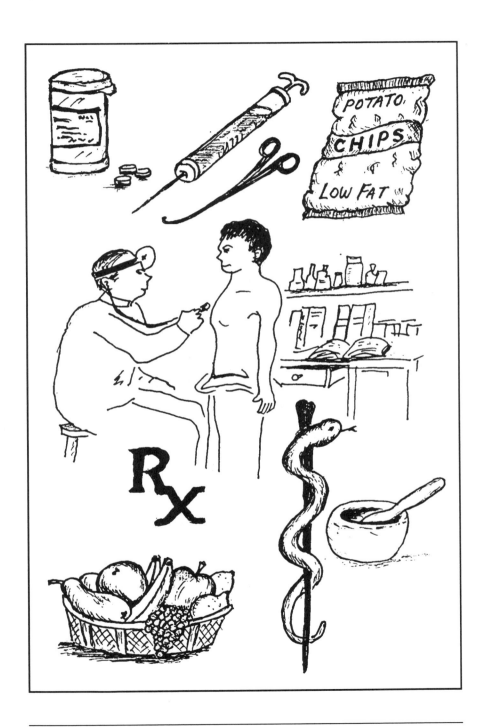

A crown is no cure for the headache.

He that dies pays all debts.

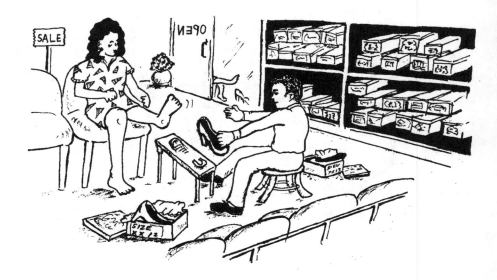

*L*et not the shoe be larger
than the foot.

*W*hat can't be cured must
be endured.

*N*othing is more harmful to health than much wine.

Fit as a fiddle.

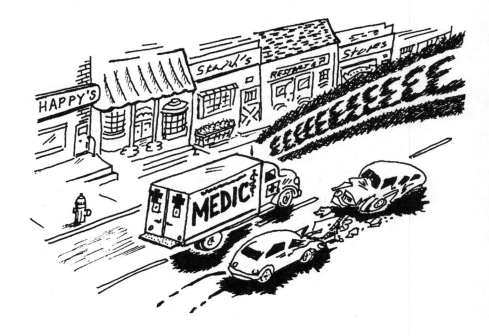

*N*ecessity has no holidays.

One hour's sleep before
midnight is worth three after.

EDUCATION

A wise man changes his mind sometimes, a fool never.

All the wit in the world is not in one head.

Great minds think alike.

I think, therefore I am.

(HOME STUDY)

3+2=5 and 4+1=5, then 3+2 must equal 4+1.

$E=MC^2$

*M*emory will diminish unless you give it exercise.

*H*unger is the instructor
of many.

*There is no royal road
to learning.*

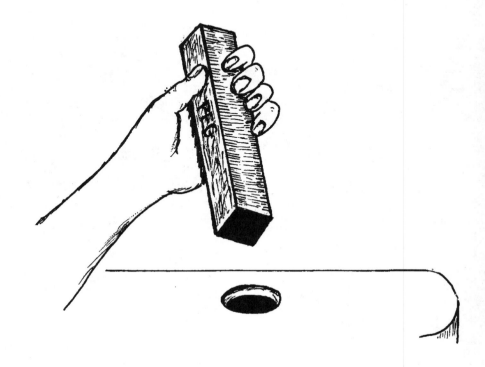

*C*ommon sense is not
so common.

The fountain of wisdom flows through books.

To acquire knowledge of human nature from men's physiognomy.

The first step to wisdom is to recognise things which are false.

*W*e live more by example
than by reason.

*A good leader produces
a good soldier.*

A wool-seller knows a wool-buyer.

*L*isten attentively to him
who has four ears.

LAW

He that will not be counseled cannot be helped.

Courts have no almanacs.

Extreme justice is often extreme injustice.

*L*et him who wishes to be
deceived, be deceived.

*E*ggs and oaths are
easily broken.

*T*o *desperate evils,*
desperate remedies.

*A*gree for the law is costly.

A word to the wise is
sufficient.

It is absurd that he who does not know how to govern himself should govern others.

*O*pportunity makes the thief.

If inwardly right do not
vex yourself.

*H*ide nothing from thy
minister, physician, and lawyer.

*J*ustice is the queen of virtues.

FORTUNE AND MISFORTUNE

A fool and his money are soon parted.

Fortune favours the brave.

Back again, like a bad penny.

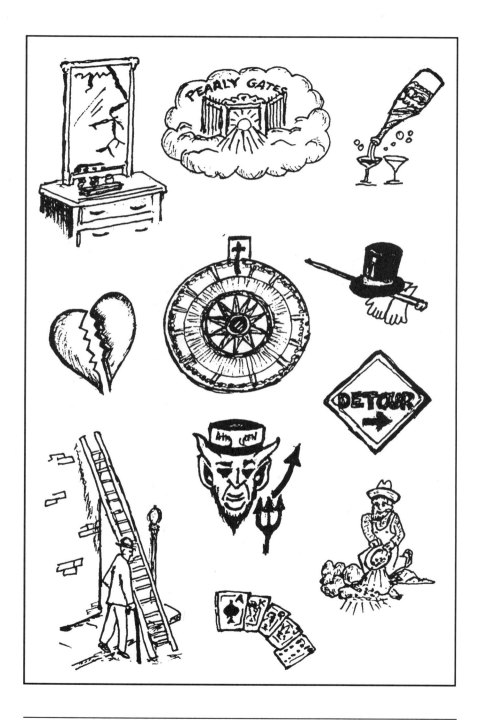

*B*e not hasty to outbid
another.

A penny saved is a
penny got.

A crooked stick can never
be made straight.

*T*hings are only worth what
cne makes them worth.

*H*e *that has gold may buy land.*

Content is better than riches.

*T*he potter is envious of the
potter, the smith of the smith.

*I*ll-fortune which cannot be
avoided is subdued by bravely
enduring.

*N*othing can be wished for
unless we have had a
preconception of it.

*B*elieve you have it,
and you have it.

*M*an can do no more than he can.

To a lucky man every land is a fatherland.

*A vice which offends no one
is not really a vice.*

Common danger produces agreement.

*F*ootsteps of fortune are slippery.

*The end of one woe is the step
to one that is to come.*

*W*hat is worth doing at all
is worth doing well.

*F*indings are keepings.

SUN AND WATER

Follow the river and you will find the sea.

Every cloud has a silver lining.

He that has a head of wax must not walk in the sun.

A full cup is hard to carry.

*R*ivers are roads which move.

*A*ttracting all like a magnet.

*N*othing more useful than
the sun and salt.

*T*he force of necessity
is irresistible.

*W*hen the winds fail,
take to the oars.

A crucial experiment.

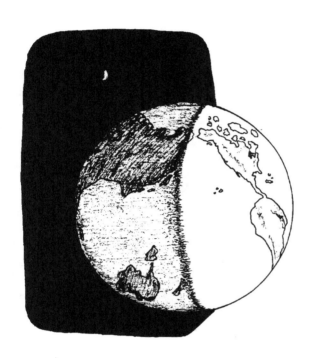

*H*alf *the world does not know
how the other half lives.*

*N*ature caused.

D*o not argue against the sun.*

A great ship asks deep waters.

We never know the worth of water till the well is dry.

ENVIRONMENT

Grass grows not on the highway.

A little bird is content with a little nest.

A mountain and a river are good neighbors.

*N*ature causing nature.

Hurry is slow.

*A*ll *nature exists in the*
very smallest things.

A plant often removed cannot thrive.

The grass withers as Fall comes on.

*A*ll things in their being are
good for something.

*T*here's safety in numbers.

*N*ature does nothing in vain.

A great deal in a small space.

*T*owns are the stink of the
human race.

*You cannot make a crab
walk straight.*

Small things have in them their own gracefulness.

LOVE AND FRIENDSHIP

A friend is easier lost than found.

Absence sharpens love, presence strengthens it.

Books and friends should be few and good.

*L*ove made the world.

*G*ive time to time.

*H*appiness seems made to be shared.

*A friend is never known
till one has need.*

*L*et not the grass grow on
the path of friendship.

*L*ove makes time pass.

*H*e is known by his
companions.

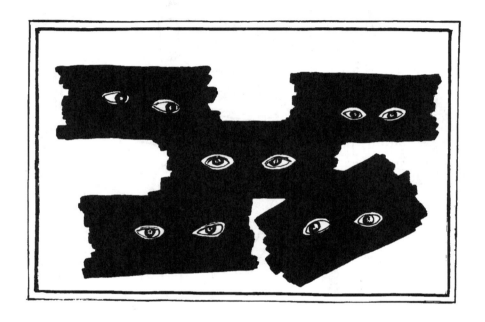

All colours will agree in the dark.

A place for everything, and
everything in its place.

*C*hoose your love, and then
love your choice.

*The good in which you let
others share becomes
thereby better.*

A man is known by his friends.

RELIGION

Better to go to heaven in rags than to hell in embroidery.

Few may play with the devil and win.

God helps those who help themselves.

*T*hey praise what they
do not understand.

A man of cruelty is God's enemy.

All is good that God sends us.

*To love your parents is the
first law of nature.*

*T*he best of all gifts is the
good intention of the giver.

To have prayed well is to
have well endeavoured.

*H*e does not cleanse himself
of his sins who denies them.

*A*bove all heights is rest.

*G*ood things are mixed with
evil, evil things with good.

*P*ray and work.

SPORTS AND GAMES

All are fellows at football.

*Everybody is wise
after the event.*

*Good to begin well,
better to end well.*

*A*n archer is known by his aim, not by his arrows.

*N*ow or never.

*L*et deeds correspond
with words.

*A*t the end of the work you
may judge of the workman.

*L*et not the praise be
before the victory.

*M*ore Irish than the
Irish themselves.

*A*llowance is to be made for
him who first attempts a thing.

Everything is good in its season.

*E*verything in accordance
to reason.

*E*veryone has judgment to sell.

*I*t is better to run back than
to run wrong.

*E*asier said than done.

*I*t may be, if it is true.

*T*he abuse of a thing does
not forbid its use.

To everyone his own form of pleasure.

Learn to depart.

HUMAN INTEREST

A mare's shoe and a horse's shoe are both alike.

Better late than never.

Fridays in the week are never alike.

*O*ne sheep follows another.

*A*t a round table there's no
dispute of place.

He that knows little
soon repeats it.

*B*ind the sack before it be full.

There is no remedy against the bite of a flatterer.

*Good words are worth much
and cost little.*

*I*t is easy to be generous with
other people's property.

*I*t is easy to add to inventions.

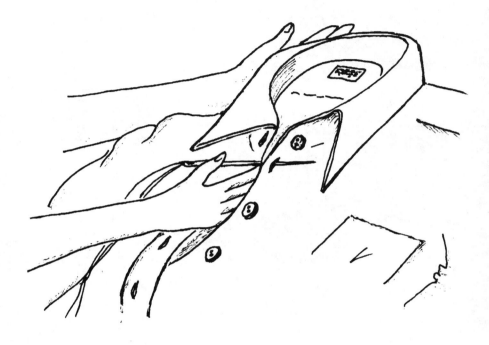

You have touched the matter
with a needle.

*N*o *tree falls at the first stroke.*

*T*he very ardent disposition
of the Scotch.

Be what you seem to be.

Daylight will peep through a very small hole.

*A*ll the world's a camera —
look pleasant, please!

INDEX

ANIMALS AND FOWL

A mouse must not think to cast a shadow like an elephant. 8

A pretty pig makes an ugly old sow. 18

All are not thieves that dogs bark at. 15

An ass is beautiful to an ass and a pig to a pig. 11

An ass is but an ass though laden with gold. 6

As the old cock crows, the young one learns. 4

Birds of a feather flock together. 14

Do not foster animals with hooked claws. 16

Do not put the saddle on the wrong horse. 20

Do not reckon your chickens before they are hatched. 12

Even the lion must defend itself against flies. 10

Every bird must hatch her own egg. 9

Every bird is known by its feathers. 22

He that would have eggs must bear with cackling. 19

He who chases two hares catches neither. 17

He that lives with wolves will learn to howl. 7

If all fools wore white caps, we should seem a flock of geese. 5

The ladder become the former. 13

What has a dog to do with a bath? 23

When the cat is away, the mice will play. 21

ART, MUSIC AND DANCE

Art consist in concealing art. 44

Art has an enemy called ignorance. 46

Criticism is easy, and art is difficult. 43

Each bird loves to hear himself sing. 48

Every land fosters some kind of art. 40

Everything ancient is to be respected. 45

Music is the incitement of love. 41

Music is the universal speech. 42

Practice makes perfect. 49

Who loves not wine, woman and song, remains a fool his whole life long. 47

CHILDREN AND FAMILIES

Boys are boys, and boys employ themselves with boyish matters. 77

Children are what you make them. 69

For that which is sweet if it be often repeated is no longer sweet. 70

God made us, and we admire ourselves. 72

Hunger is the teacher of many things. 71

It is human to err. 76

The mind remains unconquered. 68

Victory loves trouble. 75

What hands have built hands can pull down. 74

Willing or unwilling. 73

EDUCATION

A good leader produces a good soldier. 127

A wool-seller knows a wool-buyer. 128

Common sense is not so common. 122

Hunger is the instructor of many. 120

I think, therefore I am. 118

Listen attentively to him who has four ears. 129

Memory will diminish unless you give it exercise. 119

The first step to wisdom is to recognise things which are false. 125

The fountain of wisdom flows through books. 123

There is no royal road to learning. 121

To acquire knowledge of human nature from men's physiognomy. 124

We live more by example than by reason. 126

ENVIRONMENT

A great deal in a small space. 186

A plant often removed cannot thrive. 181

All nature exists in the very smallest things. 180

All things in their being are good for something. 183

Hurry is slow. 179

Nature causing nature. 178

Nature does nothing in vain. 185

Small things have in them their own gracefulness. 189

The grass withers as Fall comes on. 182

There's safety in numbers. 184

Towns are the stink of the human race. 187

You cannot make a crab walk straight. 188

FOOD AND DRINK

A common jar often holds generous nectar. 105

A mad beast must have a sober driver. 99

All bread is not baked in one oven. 100

All things require skill but an appetite. 98

Eat a bit before you drink. 102

He deserves not the sweet that will not taste of the sour. 104

He that has teeth has not bread, he that has bread has not teeth. 97

Hunger sweetens beans. 96

Those who are thirsty drink in silence. 101

Too many cooks spoil the broth. 103

FORTUNE AND MISFORTUNE

A crooked stick can never be made straight. 146

A penny saved is a penny got. 145

A vice which offends no one is not really a vice. 156

Be not hasty to outbid another. 144

Believe you have it, and you have it. 153

Common danger produces agreement. 157

Content is better than riches. 149

Findings are keepings. 161

Footsteps of fortune are slippery. 158

He that has gold may buy land. 148

Ill-fortune which cannot be avoided is subdued by bravely enduring. 151

Man can do no more than he can. 154

Nothing can be wished for unless we have had a preconception of it. 152

The end of one woe is the step to one that is to come. 159

The potter is envious of the potter, the smith of the smith. 150

Things are only worth what one makes them worth. 147

To a lucky man every land is a fatherland. 155

What is worth doing at all is worth doing well. 160

HEALTH

A crown is no cure for the headache. 108

Fit as a fiddle. 113

He that dies pays all debts. 109

Let not the shoe be larger than the foot. 110

Necessity has no holidays. 114

Nothing is more harmful to health than much wine. 112

One hour's sleep before midnight is worth three after. 115

What can't be cured must be endured. 111

HUMAN INTEREST

All the world's a camera — look pleasant, please. 249

At a round table there's no dispute of place. 237

Be what you seem to be. 247

Bind the sack before it be full. 239

Daylight will peep through a very small hole. 248

Good words are worth much and cost little. 241

He that knows little soon repeats it. 238

It is easy to add to inventions. 243

It is easy to be generous with other people's property. 242

No tree falls at the first stroke. 245

One sheep follows another. 236

The very ardent disposition of the Scotch. 246

There is no remedy against the bite of a flatterer. 240

You have touched the matter with a needle. 244

LAW

A word to the wise is sufficient. 136

Agree for the law is costly. 135

Eggs and oaths are easily broken. 133

Hide nothing from thy minister, physician, and lawyer. 140

If inwardly right do not vex yourself. 139

It is absurd that he who does not know how to govern himself should govern others. 137

Justice is the queen of virtues. 141

Let him who wishes to be deceived, be deceived. 132

Opportunity makes the thief. 138

To desperate evils, desperate remedies. 134

LOVE AND FRIENDSHIP

A friend is never known till one has need. 195

A man is known by his friends. 203

A place for everything, and everything in its place. 200

All colours will agree in the dark. 199

Choose your love, and then love your choice. 201

Give time to time. 193

Happiness seems made to be shared. 194

He is known by his companions. 198

Let not the grass grow on the path of friendship. 196

Love made the world. 192

Love makes time pass. 197

The good in which you let others share becomes thereby better. 202

PLANES, AUTOS, AND OTHER VEHICLES

Advice when most needed is least heeded. 30

Ambition and love are the wings of great actions. 28

Delays are dangerous. 35

Deliberating is not delaying. 27

He goes far that never turns. 33

Know your time. 36

Let the past be past. 26

Nothing is impossible to industry. 29

Nothing is invented and perfected at the same time. 34

Seize what is highest, and you will possess what is in between. 37

The things are most dear to us which cost us most. 32

The horseshoe that clatters wants a nail. 31

PEOPLE AND PLACES

A pair well matched. 87

An Englishman's house is his castle. 80

Country is dear, but liberty dearer still. 93

England is the paradise of women. 85

Every country has its custom. 91

Every couple is not a pair. 86

Everyone is wont to praise him who is no more. 92

Go into the country and hear what news is in town. 82

Let it be given to the most worthy. 89

Let it stand as an example. 90

Often a great man comes forth from a humble cottage. 83

One often has need of someone less than oneself. 88

We live not as we desire, but as we can. 81

What the mind of man commands to itself it obtains. 84

RELIGION

A man of cruelty is God's enemy. 207

Above all heights is rest. 213

All is good that God sends us. 208

Good things are mixed with evil, evil things with good. 214

He does not cleanse himself of his sins who denies them. 212

Pray and work. 215

The best of all gifts is the good intention of the giver. 210

They praise what they do not understand. 206

To have prayed well is to have well endeavoured. 211

To love your parents is the first law of nature. 209

SPORTS AND GAMES

Allowance is to be made for him who first attempts a thing. 224

An archer is known by his aim, not by his arrows. 218

At the end of the work you may judge of the workman. 221

Easier said than done. 229

Everyone has judgment to sell. 227

Everything in accordance to reason. 226

Everything is good in its season. 225

It may be, if it is true. 230

It is better to run back than to run wrong. 228

Learn to depart. 233

Let deeds correspond with words. 220

Let not the praise be before the victory. 222

More Irish than the Irish themselves. 223

Now or never. 219

The abuse of a thing does not forbid its use. 231

To everyone his own form of pleasure. 232

SUN AND WATER

A crucial experiment. 170

A full cup is hard to carry. 164

A great ship asks deep waters. 174

Attracting all like a magnet. 166

Do not argue against the sun. 173

Half the world does not know how the other half lives. 171

Nature caused. 172

Nothing more useful than the sun and salt. 167

Rivers are roads which move. 165

The force of necessity is irresistible. 168

We never know the worth of water till the well is dry. 175

When the winds fail, take to the oars. 169

WORK AND CHORES

A workman is known by his work. 63

After the fashion of our ancestors. 61

Any country supports the skilled workman. 55

Beneath one's dignity. 64

Elbow grease is the best polish. 52

Greatness is nothing but many small littles. 58

Injury serves as a lesson. 57

Man may bear till his back breaks. 62

Not knowledge, but practice. 59

Take things as you find them. 65

The highest seat will not hold two. 54

Things united are helpful. 56

Very great in small matters. 53

Without sweat and toil no work is brought to completion. 60

Acknowledgments

Robert Gallo

Thomas Gallo

Brion Gallo

Deborah Perkins

Lori Livingstone

Debra Bierbaum

Craig McGinnes

Pat Piper

David Glaser

Dorchester County
    Library, Cambridge,
    Maryland

Cover Design by Denise McDonald
Book Production by Whitey Schmidt
Computer Layout & Design by Michael Trawick

ABOUT THE AUTHOR

Rudy Gallo and his sketch pad are usually found where words get together for an idea. Sometimes, these meetings result in a proverb or two. He and his wife Mary live on Maryland's Eastern Shore where Rudy has a large collection of wisdom as well as sketch pads.

Order gift copies of
The Book of Illustrated Proverbs.

I would like to order _____ copies , each $12.95

Shipping (any) . . . .$ 1.75

Maryland residents add 5% sales tax . . . .$_____

     TOTAL . . . .$_____

Mail a gift copy to each of the following:

Name:_____

Address: _____

City: _____ State: _____ Zip: _____

- -

Name:_____

Address: _____

City: _____ State: _____ Zip: _____

Mail to: **Golden Seal Press**
               103 Buena Vista Avenue
               Cambridge, MD 21613
               (410) 221-6543

(This form can be copied)